T0413561

Missouri

Jim Ollhoff

Visit us at
www.abdopublishing.com

Published by ABDO Publishing Company, 8000 West 78th Street, Suite 310, Edina, Minnesota 55439 USA. Copyright ©2010 by Abdo Consulting Group, Inc. International copyrights reserved in all countries. No part of this book may be reproduced in any form without written permission from the publisher. The Checkerboard Library™ is a trademark and logo of ABDO Publishing Company.

Printed in the United States.

Editor: John Hamilton
Graphic Design: Sue Hamilton
Cover Illustration: Neil Klinepier
Cover Photo: iStock

Manufactured with paper containing at least 10% post-consumer waste

Interior Photo Credits: Alamy, AP Images, Comstock, Corbis, David Olson, Getty, Granger Collection, Gunter Küchler, Independence National Historical Park/C.W. Peale, iStock Photo, Karl Bodmer, Kristy Henderson, L. Edward Fisher/Missouri Bankers Association, Library of Congress, Mile High Maps, Mountain High Maps, Museum of Finnish Architecture, North Wind Picture Archives, One Mile Up, and Photo Researchers Inc, St. Louis Rams, St. Louis Star-Times, and Wikipedia.

Statistics: State population statistics taken from 2008 U.S. Census Bureau estimates. City and town population statistics taken from July 1, 2007, U.S. Census Bureau estimates. Land and water area statistics taken from 2000 Census, U.S. Census Bureau.

Library of Congress Cataloging-in-Publication Data

Ollhoff, Jim, 1959-
  Missouri / Jim Ollhoff.
      p. cm. -- (The United States)
  Includes index.
  ISBN 978-1-60453-660-7
  1. Missouri--Juvenile literature. I. Title.

  F466.3.O45 2010
  977.8--dc22
                            2008051716

Table of Contents

The Show-Me State

Missouri is in the middle of the United States. But back before 1845, it was the most western state. In those days, Missouri was the starting point for the trails going west. The Lewis and Clark Expedition started their exploration of the west from St. Louis. That's why Missouri is sometimes called "the Gateway to the West."

Another nickname for Missouri is the Show-Me State. There has been a long tradition in Missouri of people saying, "I won't believe it until I see it." Some people say that the phrase started with an 1899 speech made by a Missouri congressman named Willard Vandiver. He said that he was not impressed with fancy speeches or empty promises. "I'm from Missouri," he said, "and you have to show me."

The Gateway Arch in St. Louis, Missouri, is the tallest monument in the United States.

Quick Facts

Name: The state, and one of its main rivers, the Missouri River, were both named after a Native American tribe, the Missouri.

State Capital: Jefferson City, population 40,564

Date of Statehood: August 10, 1821 (24th state)

Population: 5,911,605 (18th-most populous state)

Area (Total Land and Water): 69,704 square miles (180,533 sq km), 21st-largest state

Largest City: Kansas City, population 450,375

Nicknames: The Show-Me State, or the Gateway to the West

Motto: The welfare of the people shall be the supreme law

State Bird: Bluebird

State Flower: White Hawthorn Blossom

State Tree: Flowering Dogwood

State Song: "The Missouri Waltz"

Highest Point: Taum Sauk Mountain, 1,772 feet (540 m)

Lowest Point: St. Francis River, 230 feet (70 m)

Average July Temperature: 78°F (26°C)

Record High Temperature: 118°F (48°C) on July 14, 1954, at Warsaw and Union

Taum Sauk Mountain

Average January Temperature: 30°F (-1°C)

Record Low Temperature: -40°F (-40°C) on February 13, 1905, at Warsaw

Harry S. Truman

Average Annual Precipitation: 37 inches (94 cm)

Number of U.S. Senators: 2

Number of U.S. Representatives: 9

U.S. Presidents Born in Missouri: Harry S. Truman (33rd president)

U.S. Postal Service Abbreviation: MO

Geography

The northern half of Missouri is a mostly flat area of the Midwestern United States. North of the Missouri River, the area is filled with gently rolling hills. The soil there is good for farming. Thousands of years ago, during the last ice age, glaciers bulldozed the land flat. When the glaciers melted, they left rich soil. Scientists believe that the glaciers covered the land north of the Missouri River.

The southern half of Missouri is part of an area called the Ozarks, or the Ozark Plateau. It has many more hills, mountains, deep narrow valleys, and caves. It is heavily forested.

Table Rock Lake in southern Missouri is in the Ozark Plateau.

8

Missouri's total land and water area is 69,704 square miles (180,533 sq km). It is the 21st-largest state. The state capital is Jefferson City.

In St. Louis, Missouri, a scientist looks at a seismograph recording earthquake activity. Southeastern Missouri sits on a fault line. This part of the state has a large number of earthquakes, although most are small.

The very southeast corner of Missouri is called the Bootheel area. This is because it is shaped like the heel of a boot. This area has a lot of earthquakes. A fault, or a break in the earth's crust, lies underneath the Bootheel. More than 4,000 earthquakes have been recorded in this area since 1974. Most of the earthquakes are very small, and only sensitive earthquake monitors can detect them.

A grain barge travels on the Mississippi River near Hannibal, Missouri. Barges carry a lot of freight on the state's rivers.

The Mississippi River is the eastern border of the state. The Mississippi starts in northern Minnesota and empties into the Gulf of Mexico in southern Louisiana. Big ships called barges carry freight on the river. The city of St. Louis, Missouri, is a major port on the Mississippi River.

The Missouri River is the other big river in the state. It cuts across the state, going north at Kansas City. The

Lewis and Clark.

Lewis and Clark Expedition started in St. Louis and followed the Missouri River as they explored the West.

Climate and Weather

There are many different types of weather in Missouri. The state gets drafts of cold air from Canada. It gets warm humid air coming from the Gulf of Mexico. Missouri gets dry air coming from the southwest United States.

Summers are humid and hot. Average summer temperatures can vary between 76 degrees Fahrenheit (24°C) and 90 degrees Fahrenheit (32°C). Temperatures of 100 degrees Fahrenheit (38°C) or more happen often.

In January, average temperatures can be 24 degrees Fahrenheit (-4°C) in the northern part of the state and 36 degrees Fahrenheit (2°C) in the south.

Missouri is in the path of Tornado Alley. This is an area of the United States that gets the most number of tornadoes. Missouri has an average of 26 tornadoes every year.

A tornado touches down south of Sedalia, Missouri, in 2006. Missouri is in Tornado Alley. The state gets about 26 tornadoes each year.

Plants and Animals

Before European settlers arrived, about 67 percent of Missouri was covered in forest. During that time, there were elk, bison, bears, beaver, and mink. When Europeans began to settle, the large animals left. The smaller animals, such as beaver and mink, were trapped until nearly all were gone.

Today, Missouri animals include deer, coyotes, opossums, raccoons, and skunks. Poisonous snakes include rattlesnakes and copperheads. Birds include doves, thrushes, robins, crows, hawks, owls, cardinals, blackbirds, orioles, meadowlarks, and bluebirds.

Missourians work hard to bring back some endangered animals. Environmental programs have helped many populations of deer, wild turkey, and otters.

A bright-eyed raccoon.

Opossum & Babies

Barred Owl

Red-Tailed Hawk

In Missouri's rivers and lakes, bass, pike, catfish, carp, trout, and sunfish are common.

Coneflower.

Today, about 33 percent of the state is forested. Most of the forests are in the southern part of Missouri. There are many flowers and plants in the Ozarks. The fameflower, royal catchfly, Trelease's larkspur, and the coneflower all grow in the southern part of the state. Other flowers native to Missouri are the violet, buttercup, wild rose, anemone, phlox, aster, and goldenrod.

In the forested areas of the south, common trees are oak, hickory, elm, walnut, and pine. In southeastern Missouri, there is a lot more rain, so the soil is wet much of the time. In these areas, cypress, oak, elm, and tupelo are the most common types of trees.

After once being heavily hunted, beavers have returned to Missouri's rivers and streams.

History

A people called Paleo-Indians lived in Missouri 12,000 years ago, and perhaps much earlier. They were the ancestors of the Native Americans who lived in the area when the Europeans came.

The Osage Indians lived along the Osage River. The Missouri Indians lived along the Grand and Missouri Rivers. The Otoe, Sauk, Fox, Shawnee, and Delaware Indians also lived in the state. Almost all of the Native Americans were forced out of Missouri by 1837.

A Missouri Indian, an Otoe Indian, and the Chief of the Puncas. The image was created from a painting by artist Karl Bodmer in the early 1830s.

In the mid 1700s, French miners and hunters began to settle in Missouri. Many came up the Mississippi River from New Orleans. Sainte Genevieve was settled about 1735. This is probably the oldest non-Native American settlement in Missouri. St. Louis began as a trading post in 1764.

Trappers and their pet cat travel down the Missouri River.

In 1803, the United States purchased the middle section of North America from the French. This was called the Louisiana Purchase. The entire state of Missouri was a part of the Louisiana Purchase.

President Thomas Jefferson chose Meriwether Lewis and William Clark to explore the new lands of the West. Members of the Lewis and Clark Expedition began their trip in the St. Louis area in 1804. They traveled up the Missouri River, then eventually made it to the Pacific Ocean. They returned to St. Louis in 1806. Missouri became the gateway to the West.

In 1804, Lewis and Clark set off from Missouri to explore the West.

In 1812, the area officially became the Territory of Missouri. Missouri wanted to become a state, but the issue of slavery created a lot

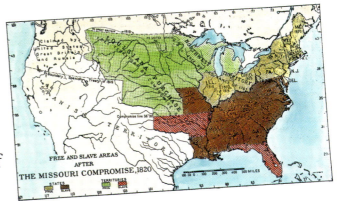

FREE AND SLAVE AREAS
AFTER
THE MISSOURI COMPROMISE, 1820

of problems. In Missouri, many people wanted slavery, while many others were against it. Those who wanted slavery won. Missouri applied for statehood with a constitution that allowed people to own other people. However, the United States federal government did not want to have any more territories that allowed slavery.

Leaders created the Missouri Compromise. This document said that Missouri could be a slave state, but the territories north and west of Missouri could not have slavery. In 1821, Missouri became the 24th state.

During the Civil War (1861-1865), many Missouri leaders wanted to side with the army in the northern states, called the Union army. Others wanted to side with the army in the southern states, called the Confederate army. About 110,000 Missourians fought on the Union side, and about 40,000 Missourians fought on the Confederate side. More than 1,000 battles were fought in Missouri.

General Nathaniel Lyon was the first Union general to be killed during the Civil War. Lyon died at the Battle of Wilson's Creek, in Missouri, on August 10, 1861.

The years during America's involvement in World War I (1917-1918) brought business to Missouri. But then the Great Depression began in 1929. This was a time when many people lost their jobs, many banks failed, and few people had money. The Great Depression hit Missouri hard, especially in

A Missouri farm family during the Great Depression.

the rural areas. During America's involvement in World War II (1941-1945), there was a demand for Missouri's agricultural and automotive products, which helped the state's economy.

After World War II, thousands of people left the rural areas and moved to the cities. Many people left farming and mining, and moved to the cities to get jobs in manufacturing.

Did You Know?

An old brick building damaged in an earthquake.

The New Madrid Earthquake was one of the largest earthquakes ever recorded in the United States. It happened near the town of New Madrid, in the Bootheel area of Missouri.

New Madrid actually had three earthquakes. The first occurred December 16, 1811. The next two quakes shook the area January 23, 1812, and a few weeks later on February 7. The last quake was the largest. Scientists estimate that it was an 8.0 on the Richter scale. People as far away as Wisconsin, Louisiana, and Washington, D.C., felt the earthquake rumblings.

The continents of the world float on giant plates. These plates are in slow, constant motion. When plates rub up against each other and stick, they can cause earthquakes. The places the plates rub against other plates are called faults. Sometimes, faults can happen far away

New Madrid was hit by several earthquakes in 1811 and 1812.

from the edge of a plate. Such a fault lies below the small town of New Madrid.

At the time of the New Madrid Earthquake, not many people lived in the area. The loss of life was small. However, scientists say it's only a matter of time before New Madrid is hit with another big earthquake.

People

George Washington Carver (1864?-1943) was one of the best scientists in the United States. Born near Diamond, Missouri, he was the son of a slave.

He was an agricultural scientist. When pests destroyed much of the cotton crop in the South, he told farmers to plant new crops. He suggested planting peanuts and soybeans, which would replenish the soil. He invented many new uses for the peanut and the sweet potato. This helped farmers sell more of their crops.

Harry S. Truman (1884-1972) was president of the United States from 1945-1953. He took office during the final months of World War II. Truman made the difficult decision to drop atomic bombs on two Japanese cities, ending the war. He led the United States through other challenging times, including the Korean War and the beginning of the Cold War. Truman was born in Lamar, Missouri.

Scott Joplin (1867?-1917) was born in Texas, but lived in Sedalia and St. Louis, Missouri. He helped develop a style of music called ragtime. This was the most commonly played music for the first 20 years of the 1900s. He studied music in college, and was called one of the best piano players in the world.

Daniel Boone (1734-1820) was a soldier and frontiersman. He spent much of his time exploring, hunting, and trapping. He was born in Pennsylvania, but became famous exploring Kentucky, and leading families to settle there. He moved to Missouri in about 1799, and finally died in St. Charles, Missouri. Many tales were told of his adventures.

Maya Angelou (1928-) was born in St. Louis, Missouri. She is one of the most famous poets in the United States. Her poetry often deals with how people mistreat others. Her poetry book *Just Give Me a Cool Drink of Water 'Fore I Diiie* was nominated for a Pulitzer Prize, the highest honor for writers. Angelou is well known for the story of her childhood, *I Know Why the Caged Bird Sings.*

Samuel Clemens (1835-1910) was a famous American writer. He is better known as Mark Twain, which is how he signed his work. Two of his most famous books were about boys in Missouri—*The Adventures of Tom Sawyer* and *The Adventures of Huckleberry Finn.* Clemens was born in the town of Florida, Missouri, and moved to Hannibal, Missouri, when he was young. His stories were filled with humor, but also made people think. He was very skilled at seeing the good and bad things going on in the world.

Cities

Kansas City, Missouri

The **Kansas City** area was settled by French fur traders in 1821. By the early 1850s, it was known as the town of Kansas, named for the Kansa, a Native American tribe. It was named Kansas City in 1889, so that people wouldn't mistake it for the Kansas Territory. Today, the city is the center for agricultural products from the surrounding area. Manufacturing and tourism are very important to the city's economy. With a population of 450,375, it is the largest city in the state.

St. Louis is the second-largest city in Missouri, with 350,759 people living there. When the populations of the surrounding cities are added, the metro area is the largest in Missouri, with more than 2.6 million people.

St. Louis was founded in 1764 by French fur traders, who set up a trading post. When steamboats began to carry people up and down the Mississippi River, the city grew rapidly.

The famous Gateway Arch is in St. Louis. The city is also home to a number of universities, including St. Louis University, Washington University, and the University of Missouri-St. Louis.

St. Louis, Missouri

The city of **Springfield** was settled in 1829. It was officially made a town in 1838. In 1870, a railroad was built between San Francisco, California, and St. Louis. The railroad went right through Springfield. That brought many people to live there. Today, the population is 154,777. Missouri State University is located in Springfield.

Park Central Square in downtown Springfield, Missouri.

The capital of Missouri is **Jefferson City**. It has a population of 40,564. The city was named for President Thomas Jefferson. Frontiersman Daniel Boone helped plan the city.

The capitol building in Jefferson City, Missouri.

Jefferson City became the capital in 1826, although it had been a trading post for a long time before that. Today, the city is a trading center for farmland and manufacturing. Lincoln University is the city's only college.

Transportation

There are more than 125,923 miles (202,653 km) of public highways in Missouri. One of the primary interstates is I-70, which stretches between St. Louis and Kansas City. The other interstate is I-44, which goes between St. Louis and Springfield, and on toward Oklahoma City, Oklahoma, in the west. I-55 goes through St. Louis, and roughly follows the Mississippi River south. I-35 travels the northwest corner of the state, coming from Des Moines, Iowa, in the north and on through to Kansas City, Missouri.

Missouri's I-70 connects St. Louis and Kansas City.

St. Louis is an important port for barge traffic on the Mississippi River. The Missouri River also goes through the St. Louis area.

The two largest airports in Missouri are Kansas City International Airport and the Lambert-St. Louis International Airport. The cities of Columbia, Joplin, and Springfield also have major airports.

A barge transports goods down the Mississippi River, passing under a modern suspension bridge at Cape Girardeau, Missouri.

Natural Resources

Agriculture has always been important in Missouri. There are more than 107,000 farms in Missouri. The state ranks second in the total number of farms in the United States (Texas is first). Soybeans, corn, wheat, and rice are important crops. Many farmers grow hay. Cotton is grown in the southern counties.

Bales of hay sit in a farm field in Cassville, Missouri.

About half of the money that comes from agriculture comes from cattle, sheep, and hogs. Many farmers also raise dairy cows, especially in the southwest. About 30 million acres (12 million ha) of land are used for agricultural purposes.

Mined minerals were important in Missouri's history. Iron ore, zinc, lead, barite, and limestone were all mined at one time. Today, mining is no longer as important as it was in the past.

At one time, the St. Joseph Lead Company was one of the top lead producing companies in the world, bringing up tons of ore each day. Today, it is a mining museum in Park Hills, Missouri.

Industry

    Missouri is a leading manufacturing state. Aircraft and transportation equipment are built in the state. Food processing, printing and publishing, and the production of chemicals bring in a lot of money, too. About 285,000 workers are employed in manufacturing jobs. Most of these jobs are in St. Louis and Kansas City.

An F/A-18 Hornet is built inside an aircraft factory in St. Louis, Missouri.

Recreation and tourism are growing parts of the economy. About 293,000 Missourians are employed in the tourist industry. Country music festivals, theaters, the beauty of the Ozarks, and the many activities in Kansas City and St. Louis bring tourists to the state.

The service industry employs the greatest number of people in Missouri. This includes people who work in restaurants, hospitals, and stores.

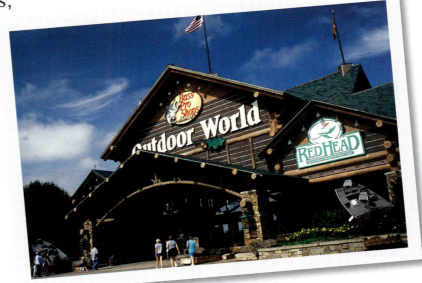

Bass Pro Shops' Outdoor World in Springfield, Missouri, is one of the world's largest sporting goods stores.

Sports

Missouri has several professional sports teams. The St. Louis Rams and the Kansas City Chiefs both play in the National Football League. The Rams won the Super Bowl in 2000. The Chiefs won the Super Bowl in 1970.

A fan of the St. Louis Rams.

In professional baseball, the Missouri teams are the St. Louis Cardinals and the Kansas City Royals. The Cardinals have won the World Series many times. The Royals won the World Series in 1985.

The St. Louis Blues play in the National Hockey League.

With 83 state parks and historic sites in Missouri, outdoor recreation is very popular. Fishing, hunting, camping, canoeing, bird watching, and wildlife viewing are available throughout the state. In the Ozarks, float fishing is popular. Float fishing means to fish from a boat while it slowly floats downstream.

Many people enjoy fishing in Missouri's lakes and rivers.

Entertainment

Gateway Arch is the tallest national monument in the United States. Nearly one million visitors take a tram to the top each year.

One of the most famous attractions in Missouri is the Gateway Arch. It is meant to symbolize that Missouri is the gateway to the West. It is 630 feet (192 m) tall, and 630 feet (192 m) wide at its base. The arch is hollow. Trams take visitors to the top, where there is an observation deck. Near the base of the arch is the Museum of Westward Expansion.

There are many amusement parks and attractions in

Missouri. Worlds of Fun in Kansas City has dozens of rides and water activities. Six Flags of St. Louis has 33 rides and 7 roller coasters. The St. Louis Zoo has provided wildlife viewing and education since 1904.

Music has always been important in Missouri.

Riders go upside down on a Six Flags of St. Louis roller coaster.

Kansas City musicians played a part in the development of jazz music. St. Louis musicians played a part in the development of blues music. Scott Joplin lived in St. Louis when he popularized ragtime music. The St. Louis Symphony is one of the oldest and best known orchestras in the United States.

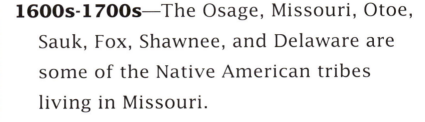

Timeline

1600s-1700s—The Osage, Missouri, Otoe, Sauk, Fox, Shawnee, and Delaware are some of the Native American tribes living in Missouri.

Mid-1700s—French miners and hunters begin to settle in Missouri.

1735—Sainte Genevieve, the first permanent European settlement in Missouri, is founded.

1764—St. Louis trading post is founded.

1803—The area that will become Missouri is included in the Louisiana Purchase.

1804—Meriwether Lewis and William Clark set out from St. Louis to explore the West.

1821—Missouri becomes the 24th state.

1861-1865—The Civil War is fought. Many battles take place in Missouri.

1929—The Great Depression begins. Many people are unemployed in Missouri.

1941-1945—The U.S. enters World War II. Missouri sends thousands of soldiers to fight.

1965—The Gateway Arch is completed in St. Louis, Missouri.

2000—The St. Louis Rams football team wins Super Bowl XXXIV.

Glossary

Civil War—The war fought between the Northern and Southern states from 1861-1865. The Southern states were for slavery. They wanted to start their own country. Northern states fought against slavery and a division of the country.

Cold War—Conflict between countries because of political differences that stops short of armed warfare.

Fault—A break in the earth's crust. A fault is often the site of earthquakes.

Glacier—A huge, slow-moving sheet of ice that grows and shrinks as the climate changes.

Korean War—A war fought from 1950 to 1953 when North Korean troops invaded South Korea. The United States and other United Nations countries joined the war to help South Korea. China sided with North Korea. A truce was signed in 1953.

Lewis and Clark Expedition—An exploration of the West, led by Meriwether Lewis and William Clark, from 1804-1806.

Louisiana Purchase—In 1803, the United States purchased the middle section of North America from the French. The entire state of Missouri was part of the Louisiana Purchase.

Ozarks—The area in the southern half of Missouri. It is heavily forested with hills, mountains, valleys, and caves.

Richter Scale—A numbered scale, from 1 (low) to 9 (high), that measures the destructiveness of earthquakes.

Tornado Alley—An area of the United States that gets many tornadoes. Missouri is in this area because cold air from Canada meets warm air from the Gulf of Mexico, causing storms.

World War I—A war that was fought in Europe from 1914 to 1918, involving countries around the world. The United States entered the war in April 1917.

World War II—A conflict across the world, lasting from 1939-1945. The United States entered the war in December 1941.

Index